Inspiration from the Beloved Hymn

Blessed Assurance

Blessed Assurance, Jesus is mine!
O What a foretaste of glory divine!

Heir of salvation, purchase of God
Born of His spirit, washed in His blood

© 2013 by Barbour Publishing, Inc.

Written and compiled by Shanna D. Gregor.

Print ISBN 978-1-62029-157-3

eBook Editions:
Adobe Digital Edition (.epub) 978-1-62029-702-5
Kindle and MobiPocket Edition (.prc) 978-1-62029-701-8

Scripture quotations marked AMP are taken from the Amplified® Bible, © 1954, 1958, 1962, 1964, 1965, 1987 by The Lockman Foundation. Used by permission.

Scripture quotations marked NKJV are taken from the New King James Version®. Copyright © 1982 by Thomas Nelson, Inc. Used by permission. All rights reserved.

Scripture quotations marked ESV are from The Holy Bible, English Standard Version®, copyright © 2001 by Crossway Bibles, a publishing ministry of Good News Publishers. Used by permission. All rights reserved.

Scripture quotations marked MSG are from *THE MESSAGE*. Copyright © by Eugene H. Peterson 1993, 1994, 1995, 1996, 2000, 2001, 2002. Used by permission of NavPress Publishing Group.

Scripture quotations marked NLT are taken from the *Holy Bible*. New Living Translation copyright© 1996, 2004, 2007 by Tyndale House Foundation. Used by permission of Tyndale House Publishers, Inc. Carol Stream, Illinois 60188. All rights reserved.

Scripture quotations marked CEV are from the Contemporary English Version, Copyright © 1995 by American Bible Society. Used by permission.

Scripture quotations marked NASB are taken from the New American Standard Bible, © 1960, 1962, 1963, 1968, 1971, 1972, 1973, 1975, 1977, 1995 by The Lockman Foundation. Used by permission.

Scripture quotations marked NCV are from the New Century Version of the Bible, copyright © 2005 by Thomas Nelson, Inc. Used by permission. All rights reserved.

Published by Barbour Publishing, Inc., P.O. Box 719, Uhrichsville, Ohio 44683, www.barbourbooks.com

Our mission is to publish and distribute inspirational products offering exceptional value and biblical encouragement to the masses.

Member of the
Evangelical Christian
Publishers Association

Printed in the United States of America.

Inspiration from the Beloved Hymn

Blessed Assurance

Blessed Assurance, Jesus is mine!
O What a foretaste of glory divine!

Heir of salvation, purchase of God
Born of His spirit, washed in His blood

BARBOUR
PUBLISHING

Blessed Assurance, Jesus is mine!
O What a foretaste of glory divine!

Heir of salvation, purchase of God
Born of His spirit, washed in His blood

CONTENTS

Blessed Assurance

Blessed assurance, Jesus is mine!
Oh, what a foretaste of glory divine!
Heir of salvation, purchase of God,
Born of His Spirit, washed in His blood.

Chorus:
This is my story, this is my song,
Praising my Savior all the day long;
This is my story, this is my song,
Praising my Savior all the day long.

Perfect submission, perfect delight,
Visions of rapture now burst on my sight;
Angels, descending, bring from above
Echoes of mercy, whispers of love.

Perfect submission, all is at rest,
I in my Savior am happy and blest,
Watching and waiting, looking above,
Filled with His goodness, lost in His love.

Fanny Crosby, 1873

Blessed Assurance, Jesus is mine!
O What a foretaste of glory divine!

Heir of salvation, purchase of Go
Born of His spirit, washed in His blood

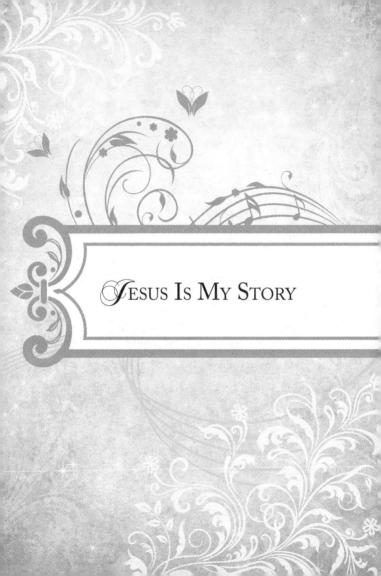

JESUS IS MY STORY

In a wealthy home some utensils are made of gold and silver, and some are made of wood and clay. The expensive utensils are used for special occasions, and the cheap ones are for everyday use. If you keep yourself pure, you will be a special utensil for honorable use. Your life will be clean, and you will be ready for the Master to use you for every good work.

2 TIMOTHY 2:20–21 NLT

Fanny Crosby, blind at six weeks of age, wrote the lyrics to "Blessed Assurance" and is credited with more than eight thousand hymns. When asked about her blindness she said, "It seemed intended by the blessed providence of God that I should be blind all my life, and I thank Him for the dispensation. If perfect earthly sight were offered me tomorrow I would not accept it. I might not have sung hymns to the praise of God if I had been distracted by the beautiful and interesting things about me."

In today's culture it's easy to discount another's contribution to society and to the kingdom of God. But every person has a specific gift and purpose— to live our lives in a way that tells Jesus' story. No matter what challenges you are facing in life, you can live above your circumstances, just like Fanny Crosby chose to do. Live each day in such a way that you tell the story of Jesus in all you say and do.

Then Jesus went to work on his disciples.
"Anyone who intends to come with
me has to let me lead. You're not in
the driver's seat; I am."

MATTHEW 16:24 MSG

For we died and were buried with Christ
by baptism. And just as Christ was raised
from the dead by the glorious power of the
Father, now we also may live new lives.

ROMANS 6:4 NLT

When Christ who is our life appears,
then you also will appear with Him in glory.

COLOSSIANS 3:4 NKJV

I know of a world that is sunk in shame,
Where hearts oft faint and tire;
But I know of a Name, a precious Name,
That can set that world on fire:
Its sound is sweet, its letters flame.
I know of a Name, a precious Name,
'Tis Jesus.

J. Wilbur Chapman

This is faith: a renouncing of everything
we are apt to call our own and relying
wholly upon the blood, righteousness,
and intercession of Jesus.

John Newton

13

*"I am the living one. I died, but look—
I am alive forever and ever! And I hold
the keys of death and the grave."*

REVELATION 1:18 NLT

❁

*"He who overcomes shall be clothed
in white garments, and I will not blot out
his name from the Book of Life; but I
will confess his name before My Father
and before His angels."*

REVELATION 3:5 NKJV

❁

*But these are written so that you may
believe that Jesus is the Christ, the Son
of God, and that by believing you
may have life in his name.*

JOHN 20:31 ESV

My Life as a Gift

Dear heavenly Father, thank You for giving me eternal life and allowing me to choose to live Jesus' story. Give me the opportunity to demonstrate His love and life in all I do. Help me remember that my life is a gift back to You each day. Amen.

Therefore, if anyone is in Christ,
he is a new creation. The old has passed
away; behold, the new has come.

2 Corinthians 5:17 esv

Now may our Lord Jesus Christ Himself
and God our Father, Who loved us and gave
us everlasting consolation and encouragement
and well-founded hope through [His] grace
(unmerited favor), comfort and encourage
your hearts and strengthen them [make
them steadfast and keep them unswerving]
in every good work and word.

2 Thessalonians 2:16–17 amp

Every character has an inward spring;
let Christ be that spring. Every action
has a keynote; let Christ be that note,
to which your whole life is attuned.

HENRY DRUMMOND

Christ alone, but we know ourselves only
by Jesus Christ. We know life and death
only through Jesus Christ. Apart from
Jesus Christ, we do not know what is our
life, nor our death, nor God, nor ourselves.

BLAISE PASCAL

*Now the law came in to increase the trespass,
but where sin increased, grace abounded all
the more, so that, as sin reigned in death, grace
also might reign through righteousness leading
to eternal life through Jesus Christ our Lord.*
ROMANS 5:20–21 ESV

❧

*No one has greater love [no one has
shown stronger affection] than to lay down
(give up) his own life for his friends.*
JOHN 15:13 AMP

A New Creation

*Father, thank You for making me
a new creation. I want to make the most
of my second chance by living my life as a
reflection of Christ. When people see me,
let them see Christ. Thank You for giving
me hope when I had no hope. Help me to
offer the hope found only in Christ Jesus
to others as You lead and guide me.
Amen.*

A warm smile is the universal
language of kindness.

WILLIAM ARTHUR WARD

Spread love everywhere you go:
First of all in your own house. . .let no
one ever come to you without leaving
better and happier. Be the living
expression of God's kindness; kindness
in your face, kindness in your eyes,
kindness in your smile, kindness.

MOTHER TERESA

Kindness is a language which the deaf
can hear, and the blind can read.

MARK TWAIN

The Gift of Salvation

These things I have written to you who believe in the name of the Son of God, that you may know that you have eternal life, and that you may continue to believe in the name of the Son of God.

1 John 5:13 NKJV

God created humankind for relationship with Him. From the time Adam and Eve sinned (Genesis 3) to today, God's goal has been to restore His relationship with His children. Through the birth, death, burial, and resurrection of His only Son, Jesus, He provided us a way back to Him.

Jesus laid down His life and trusted God to raise Him up again. Through Christ's obedience, He built a bridge for us to cross spiritually between heaven and earth, from our souls to the throne room of God, to live each day with our heavenly Father.

The greatest gift ever given—or ever received—is our salvation. It allows us to step into God's presence from death to life. Through Jesus Christ, we have assurance that we can spend this life and all eternity in His presence.

Hallelujah!

"The LORD is my strength and song,
And He has become my salvation;
He is my God, and I will praise Him;
My father's God, and I will exalt Him."

EXODUS 15:2 NKJV

My dear friends, you have always obeyed
God when I was with you. It is even more
important that you obey now while I am
away from you. Keep on working to complete
your salvation with fear and trembling.

PHILIPPIANS 2:12 NCV

For there [is only] one God,
and [only] one Mediator between
God and men, the Man Christ Jesus.

1 TIMOTHY 2:5 AMP

Three things are necessary for the
salvation of man: to know what he ought
to believe; to know what he ought to
desire; and to know what he ought to do.

St. Thomas Aquinas

The resurrection gives my life meaning
and direction and the opportunity to start
over no matter what my circumstances.

Robert Flatt

The salvation of a single soul is more
important than the production or
preservation of all the epics and
tragedies in the world.

C. S. Lewis

How will we escape if we neglect so great a salvation? After it was at the first spoken through the Lord, it was confirmed to us by those who heard, God also testifying with them, both by signs and wonders and by various miracles and by gifts of the Holy Spirit according to His own will.

HEBREWS 2:3–4 NASB

❁

"All that the Father gives Me will come to Me, and the one who comes to Me I will by no means cast out."

JOHN 6:37 NKJV

❁

And so, if we have God's Son, we have this life. But if we don't have the Son, we don't have this life.

1 JOHN 5:12 CEV

26

Washed Clean

*Jesus, thank You for the gift of salvation.
I ask that You forgive me of every sin in
my life. Wash me clean and bury the things
in my past that separated me from You
and from my heavenly Father. I ask for a
fresh start today. I choose God's will and
His ways for my life. I surrender my life
to You. Give me a clean heart and fill me
with Your Spirit today. Amen.*

"And everyone who has given up houses or brothers or sisters or father or mother or children or property, for my sake, will receive a hundred times as much in return and will inherit eternal life."

MATTHEW 19:29 NLT

The thief comes only in order to steal and kill and destroy. I came that they may have and enjoy life, and have it in abundance (to the full, till it overflows).

JOHN 10:10 AMP

God proved His love on the cross. When Christ hung, and bled, and died, it was God saying to the world, "I love you."

BILLY GRAHAM

My salvation was a free gift. I didn't have to work for it and it's better than any gold medal that I've ever won.

BETTY CUTHBERT

"In the same way that Moses lifted the serpent in the desert so people could have something to see and then believe, it is necessary for the Son of Man to be lifted up—and everyone who looks up to him, trusting and expectant, will gain a real life, eternal life."

JOHN 3:14–15 MSG

❁

If you confess with your mouth that Jesus is Lord and believe in your heart that God raised him from the dead, you will be saved.

ROMANS 10:9 ESV

God's Plan for Me

God, sometimes it is hard to do what is right. Help me to know Your Word and choose to do it each and every day. Give me a desire to do Your will and not my own. I've had a lot of dreams for my life, but I want to follow the plan You have for my life. Give me the strength to choose what is good and right. Lead me and guide me. Help me to hear Your voice and refuse to follow the voice of the stranger. Help me to trust You and lean not to my own understanding. Amen.

The greatest enemy to human souls is the
self-righteous spirit which makes men
look to themselves for salvation.

CHARLES SPURGEON

People see God every day,
they just don't recognize Him.

PEARL BAILEY

God's gifts put man's
best dreams to shame.

ELIZABETH BARRETT BROWNING

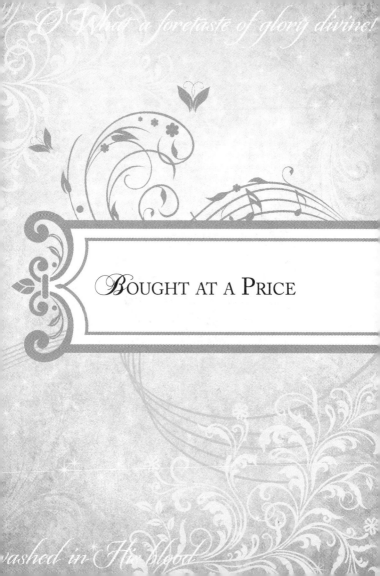

BOUGHT AT A PRICE

Again, the kingdom of heaven is like a merchant seeking beautiful pearls, who, when he had found one pearl of great price, went and sold all that he had and bought it."

MATTHEW 13:45–46 NKJV

*E*verything comes with a price. Each day we make dozens of decisions based on the cost. Sometimes it's a financial cost, but it could also be the cost of relationships, health, or faith.

Jesus counted the cost. Jesus willingly gave away His place in heaven, stepped down, and became a man, confined to a body that would ultimately experience a painful death. He submitted His own will and did the will of the heavenly Father by laying down His life. He gave a life that was only His to give so that all could experience eternal life. He paid an unimaginable price so that every man, woman, and child could receive salvation.

It cost the Father and the Son separation from one another while Jesus hung on the cross, bearing every sin that would ever be sinned. It was the highest price that could have been paid—and yet God considered each person worth it all. Every moment of pain and humiliation, the Father and Son endured for a relationship with God's beloved creation. You are valuable and considered a pearl of great price—a price God was willing to pay.

You surely know that your body is a temple where the Holy Spirit lives. The Spirit is in you and is a gift from God. You are no longer your own. God paid a great price for you. So use your body to honor God.

1 CORINTHIANS 6:19–20 CEV

He is so rich in kindness and grace that he purchased our freedom with the blood of his Son and forgave our sins.

EPHESIANS 1:7 NLT

There is never a time in the future in
which we will work out our salvation.
The challenge is in the moment;
the time is always now.

JAMES ARTHUR BALDWIN

When the Lord chooses slaves,
they become his free people. And when
he chooses free people, they become slaves
of Christ. God paid a great price for you.
So don't become slaves of anyone else.

1 Corinthians 7:22–23 cev

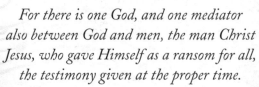

For there is one God, and one mediator
also between God and men, the man Christ
Jesus, who gave Himself as a ransom for all,
the testimony given at the proper time.

1 Timothy 2:5–6 nasb

Jesus' Sacrifice

Lord, You paid a great price for my salvation. You gave up your throne to become a man and live Your life among us. You chose to do the Father's will to bridge the gap between heaven and earth so that I might know God's great love and experience eternal life. You humiliated Yourself and became sin so that I might go free instead of bear the penalty of my own sin. Thank You for Your willingness to give Your life for mine. Help me live my life pleasing to You. Amen.

*Let the words of my mouth and the meditation of my heart be acceptable in your sight, O L*ORD*, my rock and my redeemer.*

PSALM 19:14 ESV

*"Their Redeemer is strong; the L*ORD *of hosts is His name. He will thoroughly plead their case, that He may give rest to the land, and disquiet the inhabitants of Babylon."*

JEREMIAH 50:34 NKJV

Give your life to God; He can
do more with it than you can!

Dwight L. Moody

God just doesn't throw a life preserver to
a drowning person. He goes to the bottom
of the sea, and pulls a corpse from the
bottom of the sea, takes him up on the
bank, breathes into him the breath of
life and makes him alive.

R. C. Sproul

"Whoever wishes to be first among you
shall be your slave; just as the Son of Man
did not come to be served, but to serve,
and to give His life a ransom for many."

MATTHEW 20:27–28 NASB

❁

That He would grant you, according to
the riches of His glory, to be strengthened
with might through His Spirit in the inner
man, that Christ may dwell in your hearts
through faith; that you, being rooted
and grounded in love.

EPHESIANS 3:16–17 NKJV

Give Me Faith and Peace

Heavenly Father, there are times when I am tempted to go my own way. I think my plan is right and just. Help me believe Your Word and trust Your plan. Give me eyes to see by faith where I am going when the day to day is cloudy and gray. Give me peace to walk in the path that Your Word directs as You light my way. Amen.

There are different kinds of fire; there is false fire. No one knows this better than we do, but we are not such fools as to refuse good banknotes because there are false ones in circulation; and although we see here and there manifestations of what appears to us to be nothing more than mere earthly fire, we none the less prize and value, and seek for the genuine fire which comes from the altar of the Lord.

WILLIAM BOOTH

There is nothing worth living for, unless it is worth dying for.

ELISABETH ELLIOT

Washed in His Blood

Then He took the cup, and gave thanks, and said, "Take this and divide it among yourselves; for I say to you, I will not drink of the fruit of the vine until the kingdom of God comes." And He took bread, gave thanks and broke it, and gave it to them, saying, "This is My body which is given for you; do this in remembrance of Me." Likewise He also took the cup after supper, saying, "This cup is the new covenant in My blood, which is shed for you."

LUKE 22:17–21 NKJV

A Hemopurifier is a machine that works kind of like a dialysis machine. It filters blood using thin fibers to trap and eliminate viruses from the blood of infected patients. A Hemopurifier can treat many illnesses by drawing blood from the individual, into a tube, through the machine and then sending it back into the person's body.

Sin is the deadly disease that infected all of creation on the day that Adam and Eve chose to disobey God. When Jesus gave His life, His blood provided the ultimate sacrifice. His sinless life was poured out in exchange for the sin-stained lives of anyone who willingly accepts Jesus Christ as the Lord and Savior of their life. Much like the Hemopurifier works on a physical body, spiritually, Jesus' blood purified the hearts of believers— eradicating the disease of sin.

In God's eyes an exchange was made; a transfusion occurred. We become clean and righteous in God's sight through the washing of the blood of Jesus. Through His blood we can stand in the presence of God pure and righteous because Jesus poured His life out for ours.

The blood shall be for a token or sign to you upon [the doorposts of] the houses where you are, [that] when I see the blood, I will pass over you, and no plague shall be upon you to destroy you when I smite the land of Egypt.

EXODUS 12:13 AMP

And according to the law almost all things are purified with blood, and without shedding of blood there is no remission.

HEBREWS 9:22 NKJV

But if we walk in the light, as he is in the light, we have fellowship with one another, and the blood of Jesus his Son cleanses us from all sin.

1 JOHN 1:7 ESV

This is faith: a renouncing of everything we are apt to call our own and relying wholly upon the blood, righteousness, and intercession of Jesus.

JOHN NEWTON

He drained the cup of God's wrath bone dry, leaving not a drop for us to drink.

RICHARD ALLEN BODEY

Men try to fix problems with duct tape. God did it with nails.

ANONYMOUS

*"For the life of the flesh is in the blood, and
I have given it for you on the altar to make
atonement for your souls, for it is the blood
that makes atonement by the life."*

LEVITICUS 17:11 ESV

❀

*From Jesus Christ—Loyal Witness, Firstborn
from the dead, Ruler of all earthly kings.
Glory and strength to Christ, who loves us,
who blood-washed our sins from our lives.*

REVELATION 1:5 MSG

All Things New

Father, thank You for the blood of Jesus.
I am grateful for Jesus' sacrifice. Forgive me
and make me new. Help me to remember
that my past sin and failures have
been forgiven. You no longer remember
them because they have been washed
in my Savior's blood. When guilt and
condemnation try to weigh me down,
strengthen me and remind me of the great
exchange Jesus made. I am a new creature in
Christ—You make all things new! Amen.

So Christ has now become the High Priest over all the good things that have come. He has entered that greater, more perfect Tabernacle in heaven, which was not made by human hands and is not part of this created world. With his own blood—not the blood of goats and calves—he entered the Most Holy Place once for all time and secured our redemption forever. . . . Just think how much more the blood of Christ will purify our consciences from sinful deeds so that we can worship the living God. For by the power of the eternal Spirit, Christ offered himself to God as a perfect sacrifice for our sins.

HEBREWS 9:11–12, 14 NLT

The blood of Jesus Christ has great power! There is perhaps not a phrase in the Bible that is so full of secret truth as is "The blood of Jesus." It is the secret of His incarnation, when Jesus took on flesh and blood; the secret of His obedience unto death, when He gave His life at the cross of Calvary; the secret of His love that went beyond all understanding when He bought us with His blood; the secret of the enemy and the secret of our eternal salvation.

CORRIE TEN BOOM

Jesus himself suffered outside the city gate,
so that his blood would make people holy.
HEBREWS 13:12 CEV

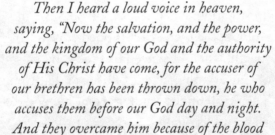

Then I heard a loud voice in heaven,
saying, "Now the salvation, and the power,
and the kingdom of our God and the authority
of His Christ have come, for the accuser of
our brethren has been thrown down, he who
accuses them before our God day and night.
And they overcame him because of the blood
of the Lamb and because of the word of their
testimony, and they did not love their life
even when faced with death."
REVELATION 12:10–11 NASB

Precious in His Sight

Lord, when I am reminded of my past mistakes, my failures, and the things that made me feel shame, help me remember all that You have done for me. Give me the courage to stand tall in Your presence and to realize and believe that I am precious in Your sight. It's not because of anything I have done. There is nothing I could do to earn Your love or my salvation. It is a gift and I receive it freely again today. Amen.

Grace isn't a little prayer you chant before
receiving a meal. It's a way to live. The law
tells me how crooked I am. Grace comes
along and straightens me out.

Dwight L. Moody

Grace does not destroy nature,
it perfects it.

Saint Thomas Aquinas

Christ is the Son of God. He died to atone
for men's sin, and after three days rose
again. This is the most important fact in
the universe. I die believing in Christ.

Watchman Nee

Walking in His Footsteps

For I have not spoken on My own authority; but the Father who sent Me gave Me a command, what I should say and what I should speak. And I know that His command is everlasting life. Therefore, whatever I speak, just as the Father has told Me, so I speak."

JOHN 12:49–50 NKJV

A four-year-old girl follows her grandfather into the field as he plants corn. He takes the end of a shovel and drops it into the loosely tilled soil then tosses several seeds of corn into the hole. The little girl squats down behind him, pokes her little finger into the dirt and drops a single kernel of corn into the hole. Children learn by mimicking the actions of adults. The same is true in spiritual growth. Jesus said, "Follow Me!"

Christ came to the earth to live a life pleasing to the Father. He led the way by example, and many of those examples are recorded in the Bible. When most adults would run children off, Jesus said, "Let the children come to Me." When others wanted to stone the woman caught in adultery, Jesus said, "He who is without sin, cast the first stone."

When you aren't certain of what you should do, you can look to the life of Jesus. He chose to follow the will of the Father. He made decisions and took actions that were pleasing in His Father's sight. Take Jesus at His words: "Follow Me!"

*[Jesus] said to them, Come after Me
[as disciples—letting Me be your Guide],
follow Me, and I will make you fishers of men!*

MATTHEW 4:19 AMP

*"And he who does not take his cross and
follow after Me is not worthy of Me.
He who finds his life will lose it, and he
who loses his life for My sake will find it."*

MATTHEW 10:38–39 NKJV

*Then Jesus went to work on his disciples.
"Anyone who intends to come with me has
to let me lead. You're not in the driver's seat;
I am. Don't run from suffering; embrace it.
Follow me and I'll show you how."*

MATTHEW 16:24 MSG

To take up the cross of Christ is
no great action done once for all;
it consists in the continual practice of
small duties which are distasteful to us.

JOHN HENRY NEWMAN

If the ultimate, the hardest, cannot
be asked of me; if my fellows hesitate
to ask it and turn to someone else,
then I know nothing of Calvary love.

AMY CARMICHAEL

And a ruler asked him, "Good Teacher, what must I do to inherit eternal life?" And Jesus said to him, "Why do you call me good? No one is good except God alone. You know the commandments: 'Do not commit adultery, Do not murder, Do not steal, Do not bear false witness, Honor your father and mother.'" And he said, "All these I have kept from my youth." When Jesus heard this, he said to him, "One thing you still lack. Sell all that you have and distribute to the poor, and you will have treasure in heaven; and come, follow me." But when he heard these things, he became very sad, for he was extremely rich.

LUKE 18:18–23 ESV

In His Footsteps

Lord, I get so lost sometimes when I forget
that I am to follow instead of lead. I want
to know where I am going. Forgive me
when I step out ahead of You and take my
own path. Give me wisdom to recognize
when I have done that. I want to live each
day in Your footsteps, going the distance
as I follow You. Help me to be a good
follower, as You lead me every day. Amen.

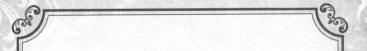

"You do not believe, because you are not of My sheep, as I said to you. My sheep hear My voice, and I know them, and they follow Me. And I give them eternal life, and they shall never perish; neither shall anyone snatch them out of My hand."

John 10:26–28 nkjv

Therefore Jesus answered and was saying to them, "Truly, truly, I say to you, the Son can do nothing of Himself, unless it is something He sees the Father doing; for whatever the Father does, these things the Son also does in like manner."

John 5:19 nasb

Whatever the particular call is, the particular sacrifice God asks you to make, the particular cross He wishes you to embrace, whatever the particular path He wants you to tread, will you rise up, and say in your heart, "Yes, Lord, I accept it; I submit, I yield, I pledge myself to walk in that path, and to follow that Voice, and to trust Thee with the consequences"? Oh! but you say, "I don't know what He will want next." No, we none of us know that, but we know we shall be safe in His hands.

Catherine Booth

Guide my steps by your word,
so I will not be overcome by evil.

PSALM 119:133 NLT

❁

And your ears shall hear a word behind you,
saying, "This is the way, walk in it," when you
turn to the right or when you turn to the left.

ISAIAH 30:21 ESV

❁

My steps have held fast to Your paths.
My feet have not slipped.

PSALM 17:5 NASB

Keep My Eyes on You

Lord, You know that sometimes the road is hard and I struggle. Life's distractions and interruptions cause me to take my eyes off You. Thank You for Your gentle promptings and Your promise never to leave me or forsake me. Give me strength for the journey and help me remain confident in my walk with You. Where You lead, I'll follow. Thank You for taking me through. Amen.

In all the world only one thing really
mattered, to do the will of the One
she followed and loved, no matter
what it involved or cost.

HANNAH HURNARD

I follow Christ: Jesus is my God—
Jesus is my Spouse—Jesus is my Life—
Jesus is my only Love—Jesus is my
All in All. Jesus is my Everything.
Because of this I am never afraid.

MOTHER TERESA

Let this be thy whole endeavor, this
thy prayer, this thy desire—that thou
mayest be stripped of all selfishness, and
with entire simplicity follow Jesus only.

THOMAS À KEMPIS

My Confidence in Christ

*Such is the confidence that we
have through Christ toward God.
Not that we are sufficient in ourselves
to claim anything as coming from us,
but our sufficiency is from God.*

2 CORINTHIANS 3:4–5 ESV

The book of Esther tells a story of a young woman who probably had every opportunity to believe God had forgotten her. She had been orphaned as a child, adopted and raised by her cousin, and living as an exile in a foreign land. Esther's confidence in God could very easily have been shaken. She could have cast her confidence aside and believed what her eyes told her about the condition of God's heart toward His people.

But she continued to trust God and grow in relationship with Him. Through her determination to hold tight to God, in His timing she became the key He used to save the very lives of her people. In spite of her hidden nationality, Esther had found favor with the king and had been chosen as his queen. She realized it was nothing she had done, but something the Lord had done on her behalf.

When you trust God for the outcome of a situation you're facing, you can choose His will and His way. You can remain confident that He will provide you with whatever you need—and the ability to do whatever He has asked you to do when the time comes. Refuse to cast your confidence aside. Hold fast to God and His promises.

*Through Christ you have come to trust
in God. And you have placed your faith
and hope in God because he raised Christ
from the dead and gave him great glory.*

1 PETER 1:21 NLT

❀

*It is better to trust in the LORD
than to put confidence in man.*

PSALM 118:8 NKJV

❀

*God is my strong Fortress; He guides the
blameless in His way and sets him free.*

2 SAMUEL 22:33 AMP

So That Others May Know You

Jesus, You are my strength and my hope. My confidence is not in man. Forgive me when I forget that. You alone are able to keep me. You gave Your all that I might live in God's promises. I give You my life and am determined to live so that others may know You. Amen.

Now this is the confidence that we have in Him, that if we ask anything according to His will, He hears us.

1 JOHN 5:14 NKJV

I will say to the LORD, "My refuge and my fortress, my God, in whom I trust."

PSALM 91:2 ESV

Now faith is the assurance (the confirmation, the title deed) of the things [we] hope for, being the proof of things [we] do not see and the conviction of their reality [faith perceiving as real fact what is not revealed to the senses].

HEBREWS 11:1 AMP

Until we know Jesus, God is merely a concept, and we can't have faith in Him. But once we hear Jesus say, "He who has seen Me has seen the Father" (John 14:9) we immediately have something that is real, and our faith is limitless.

OSWALD CHAMBERS

Faith goes up the stairs that love has built and looks out the window which hope has opened.

CHARLES SPURGEON

*And now, children, stay with Christ. Live
deeply in Christ. Then we'll be ready for him
when he appears, ready to receive him with
open arms, with no cause for red-faced guilt
or lame excuses when he arrives.*

1 John 2:28 msg

*For we who worship by the Spirit of God
are the ones who are truly circumcised.
We rely on what Christ Jesus has done for us.
We put no confidence in human effort.*

Philippians 3:3 nlt

He's Always There

Heavenly Father, thank You for always being there. Sometimes I may not feel like You're there, but by faith I know You are. You see me on both my good and bad days. No matter where I am or what is stressing me out, I can call on You for strength and assurance of my faith. I am Your child and You are my Father—and I treasure our relationship. Thank You for always being there for me. Amen.

*Dear friends, if we feel at ease in
the presence of God, we will have
the courage to come near him.*

1 John 3:21 cev

*For we have become fellows with Christ (the
Messiah) and share in all He has for us, if
only we hold our first newborn confidence and
original assured expectation [in virtue of which
we are believers] firm and unshaken to the end.*

Hebrews 3:14 amp

Justifying faith implies, not only a divine evidence or conviction that "God was in Christ, reconciling the world unto Himself," but a sure trust and confidence that Christ died for my sins, that He loved me and gave Himself for me.

JOHN WESLEY

Oh, how great peace and quietness would he possess who should cut off all vain anxiety and place all his confidence in God.

THOMAS À KEMPIS

"But I do freely admit this: In regard to the Way, which they malign as a dead-end street, I serve and worship the very same God served and worshiped by all our ancestors and embrace everything written in all our Scriptures. And I admit to living in hopeful anticipation that God will raise the dead, both the good and the bad. If that's my crime, my accusers are just as guilty as I am."

ACTS 24:15 MSG

More Than Enough

Lord, I am confident that You are more than enough for me. Through You, I can be confident of who I am. I am able to be all that You have called me to be because You have made me able. Because You live and dwell in me, I am able to handle every circumstance that comes my way. Help me to remain calm and sure of Your ability in me. Amen.

Confidence in Christ is admirable, but not effrontery and self-confidence. I am afraid of those people who are so very sure, so very confident all of a sudden, and yet have never felt the burden of sin. Be ashamed and be confounded while you lay hold on Christ, for the more He does for you the less you must think of yourself. You may very accurately measure the reality of your grace by the reality of your self-loathing.

CHARLES SPURGEON

Faith, like sight, is nothing apart from God. You might as well shut your eyes and look inside, and see whether you have sight as to look inside to discover whether you have faith.

HANNAH WHITALL SMITH

Whispers of Love

It is the Spirit who gives life; the flesh is no help at all. The words that I have spoken to you are spirit and life."

JOHN 6:63 ESV

*P*rayer is an exchange, a conversation often uttered in whispers, between God and His child. There are countless examples in the Bible of whispers from God providing direction and instruction. God called to Moses from a burning bush in the desert and gave him the assignment of his life (see Exodus 3). God whispered to Samuel while he was just a child in the middle of the night to give him a warning of things to come in the prophet Eli's house (see 1 Samuel 3). And Jesus spoke to Saul, who soon became Paul, asking Saul why he was persecuting Him (see Acts 22). In the midst of this confrontation, one of the greatest persecutors of the church became a Christian.

As you build a relationship with God and grow in knowing His voice, you learn to follow His lead. There are no perfect prayers or right ways of talking to God. He is ready and willing to hear your heart and answer the big and small questions in life. His gentle nudges and whispers of love provide instruction in reply to the questions you've asked. As you listen you will find the direction you need to live your life in a way that pleases Him.

"My sheep hear my voice, and I know them, and they follow me."

JOHN 10:27 ESV

❋

Give ear, O LORD, to my prayer; and give heed to the voice of my supplications! In the day of my trouble I shall call upon You, for You will answer me.

PSALM 86:6–7 NASB

❋

"When the Spirit of truth comes, he will guide you into all the truth, for he will not speak on his own authority, but whatever he hears he will speak, and he will declare to you the things that are to come."

JOHN 16:13 ESV

Lay My Burdens Down

*Heavenly Father, when I pray, I know
You hear me. You have promised in Your
Word to perfect all that concerns me. Today
I give all my challenges and worries to You.
I will do my best to leave them with You.
I will stand in faith and believe that You are
taking care of even the smallest challenge I'm
facing. Show me Your will and help me
to only do what You direct. Amen.*

The earnest (heartfelt, continued) prayer of a righteous man makes tremendous power available [dynamic in its working].

JAMES 5:16 AMP

The LORD is far from the wicked, but he hears the prayers of the righteous.

PROVERBS 15:29 NLT

"Hear my prayer, O LORD, and give ear to my cry; do not be silent at my tears; for I am a stranger with You, a sojourner like all my fathers."

PSALM 39:12 NASB

It may seem a little old fashioned, always to begin one's work with prayer, but I never undertake a hymn without first asking the good Lord to be my inspiration.

FANNY CROSBY

For the eyes of the Lord are upon the righteous (those who are upright and in right standing with God), and His ears are attentive to their prayer. But the face of the Lord is against those who practice evil [to oppose them, to frustrate, and defeat them].

1 PETER 3:12 AMP

Please listen when anyone in Israel truly feels sorry and sincerely prays with arms lifted toward your temple. You know what is in everyone's heart. So from your home in heaven answer their prayers, according to what they do and what is in their hearts.

2 CHRONICLES 6:29–30 CEV

A Thankful Heart

Thank You, Lord, that when I feel defeated, You are my hope. You hear my heart cries and You understand me, even when no one else does. Your words of truth from the Bible assure me—Your promises whisper to my heart and remind me of Your love for me. I will praise You with a thankful heart all of my days. Amen.

Therefore I exhort first of all that supplications, prayers, intercessions, and giving of thanks be made for all men.

1 TIMOTHY 2:1 NKJV

"This Book of the Law shall not depart from your mouth, but you shall meditate on it day and night, so that you may be careful to do according to all that is written in it. For then you will make your way prosperous, and then you will have good success."

JOSHUA 1:8 ESV

To be a Christian without prayer
is no more possible than to be
alive without breathing.

MARTIN LUTHER KING JR.

❦

I have had prayers answered—most strangely
so sometimes—but I think our heavenly
Father's loving-kindness has been even more
evident in what He has refused me.

LEWIS CARROLL

❦

None of us will ever accomplish
anything excellent or commanding
except when he listens to this whisper
which is heard by him alone.

THOMAS CARLYLE

But certainly God has heard me;
He has given heed to the voice of my prayer.

<small>PSALM 66:19 AMP</small>

He Knows Me

Heavenly Father, what an awesome privilege to speak to You in prayer. From a small whisper of concern to elaborate words of praise, You are always there. I don't have to hide anything from You. My life is open and bare before You. You know everything there is to know about me and You love me anyway. Thank You for Your presence in my life and Your unconditional love. Amen.

Prayer is more powerful than habits, heredity, and natural tendencies. It can overcome all these. It is more powerful than the forces that hold the planets in place. Prayer, though it comes from the heart of an unlearned child of God, can suspend the laws of the universe, if such be God's will, just as the sun stood still when Joshua prayed. There is no other power on earth that the enemy of souls hates and fears as he does prayer. We are told that "Satan trembles when he sees the weakest saint upon his knees."

MATILDA ANDROSS

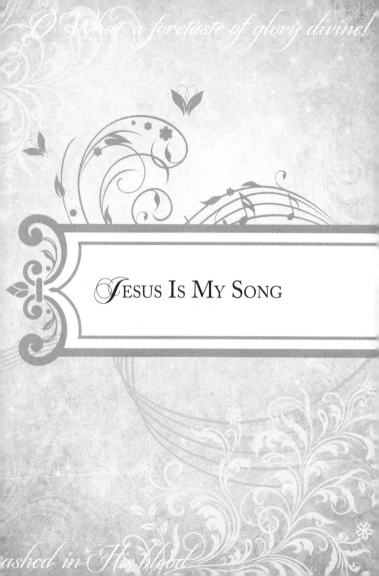

Jesus Is My Song

Sing hymns instead of drinking songs!
Sing songs from your heart to Christ.
Sing praises over everything, any excuse
for a song to God the Father in the
name of our Master, Jesus Christ.

EPHESIANS 5:19–20 MSG

Writers, composers, singers—all have tried to capture the very music that speaks to the soul of humankind. But when your soul is connected to God through acceptance of Jesus Christ, Jesus becomes your very song. A heart inhabited by Jesus cries out praise and adoration for the gift of salvation. We may struggle to understand His sacrifice, but we know He gave up His position in heaven to come to earth to lay down His very life into the hands of men who hated Him.

When you think of all He gave up to secure our salvation, it's nearly impossible to believe. He accepted death so that we could have life. He gave us peace instead of chaos. He made a way for us to experience faith in place of fear. He became the bridge that connects us to the Father, so that we could speak to the Father and come before His throne without sin.

His willingness to give Himself for you is the reason your soul can overflow with praise and live a life where Jesus really is your song!

Jesus told him, "I am the way, the truth,
and the life. No one can come to the
Father except through me."

JOHN 14:6 NLT

❀

I'm dancing the
song of my Savior God.

LUKE 1:47 MSG

❀

"Behold, God is my salvation,
I will trust and not be afraid;
for the LORD GOD is my strength and song,
and He has become my salvation."

ISAIAH 12:2 NASB

All My Praise

*Heavenly Father, let my life be a song
of praise to You. May Your Holy Spirit,
living in me, help me to express praise
to You. I pray that all I do and all I say
bring pleasure to You. I am fearfully and
wonderfully made in Your image. I desire
for my life to light the way for others
to know You. Thank You for the joy of
knowing You. Thank You for loving
me unconditionally. Amen.*

And Mary said, "My soul magnifies the Lord, and my spirit rejoices in God my Savior, for he has looked on the humble estate of his servant. For behold, from now on all generations will call me blessed; for he who is mighty has done great things for me, and holy is his name. And his mercy is for those who fear him from generation to generation. He has shown strength with his arm; he has scattered the proud in the thoughts of their hearts; he has brought down the mighty from their thrones and exalted those of humble estate; he has filled the hungry with good things, and the rich he has sent away empty. He has helped his servant Israel, in remembrance of his mercy, as he spoke to our fathers, to Abraham and to his offspring forever."

LUKE 1:46–55 ESV

Of all the earthly music, that which
reaches farthest into heaven is the
beating of a truly loving heart.

HENRY WARD BEECHER

Music is well said to be the speech
of angels; in fact, nothing among the
utterances allowed to man is felt to be so
divine. It brings us near to the infinite.

THOMAS CARLYLE

The history of a people
is found in its songs.

GEORGE JELLINEK

*Sing praises over everything,
any excuse for a song to God the Father
in the name of our Master, Jesus Christ.*

EPHESIANS 5:20 MSG

✿

*Then Moses and the people of Israel sang this
song to the LORD, saying, "I will sing to the
LORD, for he has triumphed gloriously; the
horse and his rider he has thrown into the sea."*

EXODUS 15:1 ESV

✿

*"Write down this song for yourselves, and
teach it to the children of Israel; put it in their
mouths, that this song may be a witness for
Me against the children of Israel."*

DEUTERONOMY 31:19 NKJV

Your Song in My Heart

Lord, You have put Your song in my heart.
Some days it is quiet and soft; other days
it is loud like a marching band. Your joy
bubbles up through me and is my strength
in the bright sunlight and during the
dark nights. Help me sing the song You've
given me each and every day. May Your
song living in me touch the hearts of every
person around me. Amen.

I will sing to the LORD as long as I live.
I will praise my God to my last breath!

PSALM 104:33 NLT

Let the word of Christ dwell in you richly in all
wisdom, teaching and admonishing one another
in psalms and hymns and spiritual songs,
singing with grace in your hearts to the Lord.

COLOSSIANS 3:16 NKJV

Certain thoughts are prayers. There are
moments when, whatever be the attitude
of the body, the soul is on its knees.

VICTOR HUGO

There is nothing in the world
so much like prayer as music is.

WILLIAM P. MERRI

There is in souls a sympathy with sounds:
And as the mind is pitch'd
the ear is pleased
With melting airs, or martial,
brisk or grave;
Some chord in unison with what we hear
Is touch'd within us, and the heart replies.

WILLIAM COWPER

God holds me head and shoulders
above all who try to pull me down.
I'm headed for his place to offer anthems
that will raise the roof! Already I'm singing
God-songs; I'm making music to GOD.

PSALM 27:6 MSG

I'm thanking you, God, from a full heart,
I'm writing the book on your wonders.
I'm whistling, laughing, and jumping for joy;
I'm singing your song, High God.

PSALM 9:1–2 MSG

My Hope of Heaven

For we know that when this earthly tent we live in is taken down (that is, when we die and leave this earthly body), we will have a house in heaven, an eternal body made for us by God himself and not by human hands.

2 CORINTHIANS 5:1 NLT

God created us humans as eternal beings; time does not stop with physical death. Often when a loved one dies, the grieving family members turn their thoughts to heaven and God's promise of eternal life. It gives a peace knowing that someday they will see them again and be united for eternity in heaven. Christian apologist and writer C. S. Lewis said, "To enter heaven is to become more human than you ever succeeded in being on earth; to enter hell, is to be banished from humanity."

Paul compares the Christian life to a race, with the winner taking the prize of eternal life (Philippians 3:14). As believers, our focus should not be on the things of this life—but on our future with Jesus Christ. Paul encourages believers to live for the heavenly prize rather than the rewards on earth.

Heaven is the final destination for every person who accepts Christ and lives for Him, and God desires for all to know Him. This life is short in comparison to all eternity, but how we choose to live it makes an impact on those around us. We can live each day with God's blessing and favor, knowing that we bring pleasure to Him in our thoughts, feelings, and behavior.

*In My Father's house there are many
dwelling places (homes). If it were not so,
I would have told you; for I am going
away to prepare a place for you.*

JOHN 14:2 AMP

*"For God so loved the world that He gave His
only begotten Son, that whoever believes in Him
should not perish but have everlasting life."*

JOHN 3:16 NKJV

*That is what the Scriptures mean when
they say, "No eye has seen, no ear has heard,
and no mind has imagined what God has
prepared for those who love him."*

1 CORINTHIANS 2:9 NLT

When I get to heaven, the first
face that shall ever gladden my
sight will be that of my Savior.

FANNY CROSBY

To go to heaven, fully to enjoy God,
is infinitely better than the most
pleasant accommodations here.

JONATHAN EDWARDS

Next, all of us who are still alive will be taken up into the clouds together with them to meet the Lord in the sky. From that time on we will all be with the Lord forever.

1 Thessalonians 4:17 cev

✿

And night will be no more. They will need no light of lamp or sun, for the Lord God will be their light, and they will reign forever and ever.

Revelation 22:5 esv

✿

This Christian life is a great mystery, far exceeding our understanding, but some things are clear enough: He appeared in a human body, was proved right by the invisible Spirit, was seen by angels. He was proclaimed among all kinds of peoples, believed in all over the world, taken up into heavenly glory.

1 Timothy 3:16 msg

My Eternal Home

Lord, heaven is my home for all eternity.
When I think about my forever home and
all that heaven is to me, it helps me to
realize that the time here on earth is short.
Help me remember to make these days on
earth count, but to also live each day with
the big picture of eternity in mind. May
I take time for the things that will last—
relationships with family and friends,
and my relationship with You. Amen.

The glory of God made the city bright.
It was dazzling and crystal clear like a
precious jasper stone. The city had a high
and thick wall with twelve gates, and each
one of them was guarded by an angel.

REVELATION 21:11–12 CEV

But friends, that's exactly who we are:
children of God. And that's only the
beginning. Who knows how we'll end up!
What we know is that when Christ is openly
revealed, we'll see him—and in seeing him,
become like him. All of us who look forward
to his Coming stay ready, with the glistening
purity of Jesus' life as a model for our own.

1 JOHN 3:2–3 MSG

Through all eternity to thee,
A joyful song I'll raise;
for oh! Eternity's too short
to utter all thy praise.

JOSEPH ADDISON

Love is indestructible.
Its holy flame forever burneth;
from heaven it came,
to heaven it returneth.

ROBERT SOUTHEY

All this and heaven, too.

MATTHEW HENRY

They also said, "Men of Galilee, why do you stand looking into the sky? This Jesus, who has been taken up from you into heaven, will come in just the same way as you have watched Him go into heaven."

ACTS 1:11 NASB

Then Micaiah said, "Therefore hear the word of the LORD: I saw the LORD sitting on His throne, and all the host of heaven standing on His right hand and His left."

2 CHRONICLES 18:18 NKJV

Heaven Here and Now

Father, heaven is not a faraway place, but my eternal home. Through my relationship with You, I can experience heaven in my heart today. Time in Your presence through prayer allows me a small glimpse of the joy I will know in my forever home. Help me to keep an eternal focus as I walk out this short journey on earth, knowing I will spend eternity with You. Amen.

There are heavenly bodies and earthly bodies,
but the glory of the heavenly is of one kind,
and the glory of the earthly is of another.
There is one glory of the sun, and another
glory of the moon, and another glory of
the stars; for star differs from star in glory.
So is it with the resurrection of the dead.
What is sown is perishable; what is raised
is imperishable. It is sown in dishonor; it is
raised in glory. It is sown in weakness; it is
raised in power. It is sown a natural body;
it is raised a spiritual body. If there is a
natural body, there is also a spiritual body.

1 CORINTHIANS 15:40–44 ESV

God is the same God in heaven as on earth, but I shall not be the same man.

RICHARD BAXTER

Why should my heart be fixed where my home is not? Heaven is my home; God in Christ is all my happiness: and where my treasure is, there my heart should be.

MARGARET CHARLTON BAXTER

Things learned on earth,
we shall practice in heaven.

ROBERT BROWNING

Thus it is written, "The first man Adam became a living being"; the last Adam became a life-giving spirit. But it is not the spiritual that is first but the natural, and then the spiritual. The first man was from the earth, a man of dust; the second man is from heaven. As was the man of dust, so also are those who are of the dust, and as is the man of heaven, so also are those who are of heaven. Just as we have borne the image of the man of dust, we shall also bear the image of the man of heaven.

1 CORINTHIANS 15:45–49 ESV

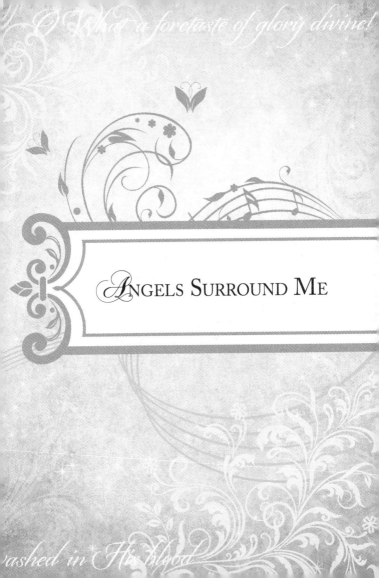

ANGELS SURROUND ME

*Do not neglect to show hospitality
to strangers, for by this some have
entertained angels without knowing it.*

HEBREWS 13:2 NASB

Songs have been written and stories have been told since the beginning of time, recording the influence of God's angels. Maybe you have even personally felt a supernatural intervention in your own life or experienced a visit from someone that you thought might have been an angel.

The Bible is full of stories of angelic encounters. Angels protected Daniel's very life in the lions' den by shutting the hungry beasts' mouths (Daniel 6:22). An angel announced the promise of children to their parents: Abraham and Sarah, John and Elizabeth, and Joseph and Mary. Angels warned Lot of the pending destruction of Sodom and Gomorrah and Joseph of Herod's plan to kill the baby Jesus (Matthew 2:13).

Still today stories are shared of divine intervention in the lives of God's people. Miraculous stories of those who supernaturally avoided tragedy or survived a terrible ordeal much like the story of Paul's escape from prison at the hand of His angel (Acts 12:1–9).

God's Word is very clear that angels are sent to minister to God's children. They often provide protection, intervention, encouragement, or instruction. They are not to be worshipped, like God, but to be received as messengers from God's throne, doing the Lord's good pleasure on our behalf.

No evil will befall you, nor will any plague come near your tent. For He will give His angels charge concerning you, to guard you in all your ways. They will bear you up in their hands, that you do not strike your foot against a stone.

PSALM 91:10–12 NASB

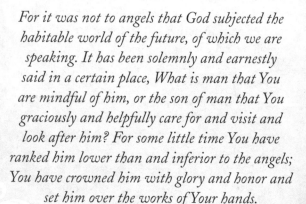

For it was not to angels that God subjected the habitable world of the future, of which we are speaking. It has been solemnly and earnestly said in a certain place, What is man that You are mindful of him, or the son of man that You graciously and helpfully care for and visit and look after him? For some little time You have ranked him lower than and inferior to the angels; You have crowned him with glory and honor and set him over the works of Your hands.

HEBREWS 2:5–7 AMP

In old days there were angels who came and took men by the hand and led them away from the city of destruction. We see no white-winged angels now. But yet men are led away from threatening destruction: a hand is put into theirs, which leads them forth gently toward a calm and bright land, so that they look no more backward; and the hand may be a little child's.

George Eliot

Whether we are filled with joy
or grief, our angels are close to us,
speaking to our hearts of God's love.

Eileen Elias Freeman

Therefore, angels are only servants—
spirits sent to care for people who
will inherit salvation.

HEBREWS 1:14 NLT

Suddenly, the angel was joined by a vast
host of others—the armies of heaven—
praising God and saying, "Glory to God
in highest heaven, and peace on earth to
those with whom God is pleased." When the
angels had returned to heaven, the shepherds
said to each other, "Let's go to Bethlehem!
Let's see this thing that has happened,
which the Lord has told us about."

LUKE 2:13–15 NLT

The angel of the LORD encamps all around
those who fear Him, and delivers them.

PSALM 34:7 NKJV

Heavenly Encouragement

*Father, thank You for sending Your angels to
minister to me. You have promised in Your
Word that they will go before me and keep me
in all my ways. They provide safety in times of
danger and encouragement in times of despair.
Although I may never see them or experience
them physically, help me to remember and
know that they are there. Amen.*

"I am sending an angel before you to protect you on your journey and lead you safely to the place I have prepared for you. Pay close attention to him, and obey his instructions. Do not rebel against him, for he is my representative, and he will not forgive your rebellion. But if you are careful to obey him, following all my instructions, then I will be an enemy to your enemies, and I will oppose those who oppose you."

EXODUS 23:20–22 NLT

"See that you do not despise one of these little ones. For I tell you that in heaven their angels always see the face of my Father who is in heaven."

MATTHEW 18:10 ESV

Angels descending, bring from above,
echoes of mercy, whispers of love.

FANNY J. CROSBY

Hush, my dear, lie still and slumber!
Holy angels guard thy bed!
Heavenly blessings without number
Gently falling on thy head.

ISAAC WATTS

All lost things are in
the angels' keeping, Love;
No past is dead for us,
but only sleeping, Love.

HELEN (FISKE) HUNT JACKSON

The two men said to Lot, "Do you have any other family here? Sons, daughters—anybody in the city? Get them out of here, and now! We're going to destroy this place. The outcries of victims here to GOD are deafening; we've been sent to blast this place into oblivion."

GENESIS 19:12–13 MSG

❁

"I tell you for certain that you will see heaven open and God's angels going up and coming down on the Son of Man."

JOHN 1:51 CEV

❁

"Don't you realize that I could ask my Father for thousands of angels to protect us, and he would send them instantly?"

MATTHEW 26:53 NLT

Angels Unawares

Lord, there are times in my life that I have experienced supernatural intervention— times I may not have even recognized it. Thank You for all the times that You have sent Your messengers—Your angels in my life. There are many times, unknown to me, that they have shielded me from the enemy or brought answers to my prayers. Thank You! Amen.

*And being warned in a dream not to
return to Herod, they departed to their
own country by another way. Now when
they had departed, behold, an angel of the
Lord appeared to Joseph in a dream and
said, "Rise, take the child and his mother,
and flee to Egypt, and remain there until
I tell you, for Herod is about to search
for the child, to destroy him."*

MATTHEW 2:12–13 ESV

*They laid hands on the apostles and put
them in a public jail. But during the night
an angel of the Lord opened the gates of the
prison, and taking them out he said, "Go,
stand and speak to the people in the temple
the whole message of this Life."*

ACTS 5:18–20 NASB

Watching and Waiting

*You will keep him in perfect peace,
whose mind is stayed on You,
because he trusts in You."*

Isaiah 26:3 NKJV

For nine long months, an expectant mother awaits the arrival of her baby. Physical, mental, and emotional preparations all help her focus on the main thing: the baby growing inside her womb. She has a focal point to a sometimes all-consuming goal: to welcome the baby into the world. As Christians, we have another goal in mind—to focus on Jesus Christ and eagerly await His return.

This world is temporary; heaven is the final destination for all who have accepted Christ as their Lord and Savior. This life seems very real—it's tangible. The minutes tick by, and we can easily become consumed by living in the moment. Challenges, problems, difficulties, and hardships can be overwhelming, drawing all our attention to this life on earth. The pressures can cause distraction, causing us take our eyes off the focal point, eventually losing sight of the big picture.

The Bible tells believers to watch and wait for the time when Christ calls them home. Today, focus on the strength that comes from the one and only Savior of the world. How do we cultivate an expectant heart? By reading the Bible, spending time in prayer, and drawing strength from fellowship with other believers. Come, Lord Jesus, come!

And He will send out His angels with a loud trumpet call, and they will gather His elect (His chosen ones) from the four winds, [even] from one end of the universe to the other.

MATTHEW 24:31 AMP

"Remember the former things of old, for I am God, and there is no other; I am God, and there is none like Me, declaring the end from the beginning, and from ancient times things that are not yet done, saying, 'My counsel shall stand, and I will do all My pleasure.'"

ISAIAH 46:9–10 NKJV

But of that [exact] day and hour no one knows, not even the angels of heaven, nor the Son, but only the Father. As were the days of Noah, so will be the coming of the Son of Man.

MATTHEW 24:36–37 AMP

You never know how much you
really believe anything until its
truth or falsehood becomes a matter
of life and death to you.

C. S. Lewis

He whose head is in heaven need
not fear to put his feet into the grave.

Matthew Henry

When they had crossed, Elijah said to Elisha, "Ask what I shall do for you, before I am taken from you." And Elisha said, "Please let there be a double portion of your spirit on me." And he said, "You have asked a hard thing; yet, if you see me as I am being taken from you, it shall be so for you, but if you do not see me, it shall not be so." And as they still went on and talked, behold, chariots of fire and horses of fire separated the two of them. And Elijah went up by a whirlwind into heaven. And Elisha saw it and he cried, "My father, my father! The chariots of Israel and its horsemen!" And he saw him no more.

2 KINGS 2:9–12 ESV

Ready for His Return

Heavenly Father, this life is full of distractions. I can often get too busy doing too many good things that I lose focus on the promise of Christ's return. I want to be ready when You call us home. I don't want to be doing things—I want to be doing the right things. Help me to be watchful and ready for His return. Amen.

*"Therefore you also must be ready,
for the Son of Man is coming at
an hour you do not expect."*

MATTHEW 24:44 ESV

*Everyone has to die once, then face the
consequences. Christ's death was also a
one-time event, but it was a sacrifice that
took care of sins forever. And so, when he
next appears, the outcome for those eager
to greet him is, precisely, salvation.*

HEBREWS 9:27–28 MSG

*"For the Son of Man will come with his
angels in the glory of his Father and will
judge all people according to their deeds."*

MATTHEW 16:27 NLT

The Christian life is a life that
consists of following Jesus.

A. W. PINK

When we learn to say a deep, passionate
yes to the things that really matter. . .then
peace begins to settle onto our lives like
golden sunlight sifting to a forest floor.

THOMAS KINKADE

*You are not missing out on any blessings,
as you wait for him to return.*

1 Corinthians 1:7 cev

❀

*So that you may approve the things
that are excellent, in order to be sincere
and blameless until the day of Christ.*

Philippians 1:10 nasb

❀

*Finally, there is laid up for me the crown of
righteousness, which the Lord, the righteous Judge,
will give to me on that Day, and not to me only
but also to all who have loved His appearing.*

2 Timothy 4:8 nkjv

An Outward Focus

Lord, time is short and Your return is close.
I can get so caught up in what is going on
in my own life that I forget about others.
Help me to become more "others focused."
Give me words to speak and opportunities to
point others to You so that they will also be
watching and waiting for Your return. Amen.

*But we are citizens of the state
(commonwealth, homeland) which is in
heaven, and from it also we earnestly
and patiently await [the coming of] the
Lord Jesus Christ (the Messiah) [as] Savior.*

PHILIPPIANS 3:20 AMP

*When the chief Shepherd appears, you will
receive the unfading crown of glory.*

1 PETER 5:4 ESV

*But you, dear friends, carefully build
yourselves up in this most holy faith
by praying in the Holy Spirit, staying
right at the center of God's love, keeping
your arms open and outstretched, ready
for the mercy of our Master, Jesus Christ.
This is the unending life, the real life!*

JUDE 1:20–21 MSG

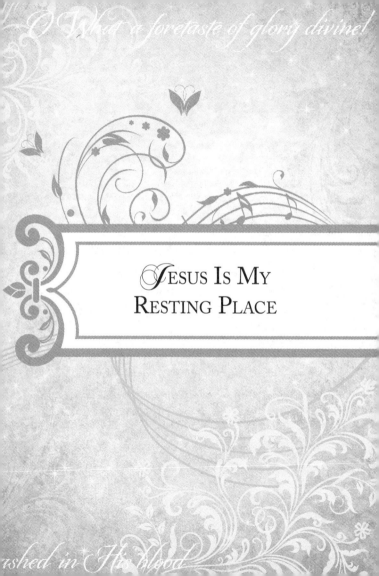

O What a foretaste of glory divine!

Jesus Is My Resting Place

shed in His blood

P eace I leave with you; my peace I give to you. Not as the world gives do I give to you. Let not your hearts be troubled, neither let them be afraid."

JOHN 14:27 ESV

The world moves at a fast pace. Schedules are full, and most people are busier than ever. The chaos of family relationships, ongoing economic concerns, and a host of other issues today lend to frustrations and constant interruptions. It's easy to fall into the trap of worry in your life and in the lives of friends and family. It leaves little time for rest and relaxation.

Just as a time of rest for your physical body is vital to your health, rest for your spirit is also important. The worries and concerns of life can weigh heavy sometimes, but Jesus encourages us to give our concerns to Him. So imagine packing up all your worries, putting them in a suitcase, and shipping them off to Him. He will never return to sender.

The Prince of Peace makes His peace available to everyone who believes in Him (Isaiah 9:6; John 14:27). When you make time for quiet moments with your Savior, His peace provides a rest for your soul that allows you the assurance you can remain steadfast and secure in the midst of the most difficult circumstances. When your soul is anchored in Him, He becomes the very source of peace.

"Take My yoke upon you and learn from Me, for I am gentle and lowly in heart, and you will find rest for your souls."

MATTHEW 11:29 NKJV

The LORD is my shepherd; I shall not want.
He makes me lie down in green pastures.
He leads me beside still waters.
He restores my soul.

PSALM 23:1–3 ESV

Thou hast created us for Thyself, and our
heart is not quiet until it rests in Thee.

SAINT AUGUSTINE

The soul on earth is an immortal guest,
compelled to starve at an unreal feast;
a pilgrim panting for the rest to come;
an exile, anxious for his native home.

HANNAH MORE

Our rest lies in looking to
the Lord, not to ourselves.

WATCHMAN NEE

God said, "My presence will go with you.
I'll see the journey to the end."

EXODUS 33:14 MSG

❀

"I am leaving you with a gift—
peace of mind and heart. And the peace
I give is a gift the world cannot give.
So don't be troubled or afraid."

JOHN 14:27 NLT

He Supplies Peace

Jesus, my world moves at a fast pace every day. You are my place of peace. When the world crowds in and I can't find rest, please gently remind me to take a breath and get away to a place where I can spend time with You. Wash me in a shower of Your presence and infuse me with Your strength. Help me to remember I can't do this on my own—and I don't have to. Today I'm inviting You to do my life with me. Amen.

God gives peace, and he raised our Lord Jesus Christ from death. Now Jesus is like a Great Shepherd whose blood was used to make God's eternal agreement with his flock. I pray that God will make you ready to obey him and that you will always be eager to do right. May Jesus help you do what pleases God. To Jesus Christ be glory forever and ever! Amen.

HEBREWS 13:20–21 CEV

Great peace have they who love Your law; nothing shall offend them or make them stumble.

PSALM 119:165 AMP

And He said to them, "Come aside by yourselves to a deserted place and rest a while." For there were many coming and going, and they did not even have time to eat.

MARK 6:31 NKJV

Once I knew what it was to rest upon the rock of God's promises, and it was indeed a precious resting place, but now I rest in His grace. He is teaching me that the bosom of His love is a far sweeter resting-place than even the rock of His promises.

HANNAH WHITALL SMITH

God will never, never, never let us down if we have faith and put our trust in Him. He will always look after us. So we must cleave to Jesus. Our whole life must simply be woven into Jesus.

MOTHER TERESA

"Live in me. Make your home in me just as I do in you. In the same way that a branch can't bear grapes by itself but only by being joined to the vine, you can't bear fruit unless you are joined with me."

JOHN 15:4 MSG

My victory and honor come from God alone. He is my refuge, a rock where no enemy can reach me.

PSALM 62:7 NLT

Soul Restoration

Jesus, just as I need physical rest,
I need times of refreshing in my soul.
Sometimes I forget that I need that time
away with You to rest and refuel. Remind
me to get away with You and refuel my
spirit. I know You will whisper peace to
my heart and restore my soul when I
spend time with You. Amen.

*Thus says the LORD: "Stand by the roads,
and look, and ask for the ancient paths,
where the good way is; and walk in it,
and find rest for your souls. But they said,
'We will not walk in it.'"*

JEREMIAH 6:16 ESV

*My darling, I am yours, and you are mine,
as you feed your sheep among the lilies.*

SONG OF SONGS 2:16 CEV

Filled with His Goodness

*Every good gift and every perfect gift
is from above, and comes down from the
Father of lights, with whom there is no
variation or shadow of turning.*

JAMES 1:17 NKJV

When a witness in a court case gives an account of what he saw, he provides a record of what was said and done. When we share our stories of God's miraculous intervention in our lives, we're testifying on God's behalf much like a witness in a court of law.

God encourages each generation to tell the next generation of His miraculous intervention in the lives of His people. The Bible is full of stories of how God delivered His people from the hands of their enemies, gave them water in the desert, opened the Red Sea so they could cross on dry land, and brought them into the Promised Land. During Jesus' time on the earth He healed the sick, raised the dead, and showered those who would receive Him with His Father's goodness—mercy and grace.

God stories are still powerful today. When someone shares the story of God's goodness in his or her life, it builds faith, increases hope, removes limits, and inspires listeners to believe that what God can do for one—He will do for another. God's sons and daughters are created in His image—to reflect His likeness. God is everything good, and so His children are also filled with His goodness. Share His mercy, goodness, and love with the lives of those He brings into your life today.

*What shall I render to the L*ORD
for all His benefits toward me?

PSALM 116:12 NASB

*[What, what would have become of me] had
I not believed that I would see the Lord's
goodness in the land of the living!*

PSALM 27:13 AMP

*"Now therefore, arise, O L*ORD *God,
to Your resting place, You and the ark of
Your strength. Let Your priests, O L*ORD
*God, be clothed with salvation, and let
Your saints rejoice in goodness."*

2 CHRONICLES 6:41 NKJV

Receive every day as a resurrection from death, as a new enjoyment of life; meet every rising sun with such sentiments of God's goodness, as if you had seen it, and all things, new-created upon your account: and under the sense of so great a blessing, let your joyful heart praise and magnify so good and glorious a Creator.

WILLIAM LAW

After the knowledge of, and obedience to, the will of God, the next aim must be to know something of His attributes of wisdom, power, and goodness as evidenced by His handiwork.

JAMES PRESCOTT JOULE

And he said, "I will make all my goodness pass before you and will proclaim before you my name 'The LORD.' And I will be gracious to whom I will be gracious, and will show mercy on whom I will show mercy.'"

EXODUS 33:19 ESV

Oh, thank GOD—he's so good! His love never runs out. All of you set free by GOD, tell the world! Tell how he freed you from oppression, then rounded you up from all over the place, from the four winds, from the seven seas.

PSALM 107:1 MSG

God's Goodness

God, there is a lot of ugliness and evil in this world. I see it everywhere I turn. Sometimes it can cause me to become discouraged and distraught. But You are good. Open my eyes to Your goodness. Let me see Your goodness in mankind. Help me to celebrate it when I see it—and encourage others when Your goodness is evident in their lives. Thank You for Your promise for Your goodness and mercy follows me all my days. Amen.

How great is the goodness you have stored up for those who fear you. You lavish it on those who come to you for protection, blessing them before the watching world.

PSALM 31:19 NLT

But later, Israel will turn back to the LORD their God and to David their king. At that time they will come to the LORD with fear and trembling, and he will be good to them.

HOSEA 3:5 CEV

Of all virtues and dignities of the mind, goodness is the greatest, being the character of the Deity; and without it, man is a busy, mischievous, wretched thing.

Francis Bacon

We are kept all as securely in love in woe as in weal, by the goodness of God.

Julian of Norwich

Nobody ever got anything from God on the grounds that he deserved it. Haven fallen, man deserves only punishment and death. So if God answers prayer it's because God is good. From His goodness, His lovingkindness, His good-natured benevolence, God does it! That's the source of everything.

A. W. Tozer

*For everything created by God is good,
and nothing is to be rejected if
it is received with gratitude.*

1 TIMOTHY 4:4 NASB

*Every good gift and every perfect (free, large,
full) gift is from above; it comes down from
the Father of all [that gives] light, in [the
shining of] Whom there can be no variation
[rising or setting] or shadow cast by His
turning [as in an eclipse].*

JAMES 1:17 AMP

Being a Blessing

Heavenly Father, all the good in my life is from You. I desire to be a reflection of Your goodness in the lives of those around me. Show me how to seize each opportunity to be a light of Your goodness to my family, friends, and even strangers. No matter what I'm dealing with in my own life, help me to realize that others are also navigating a journey of their own. Help me to be a blessing to them. Amen.

" *'For I am the* LORD *your God.*
You shall therefore consecrate yourselves,
and you shall be holy; for I am holy.' "

LEVITICUS 11:44 NKJV

Truly God is good to Israel,
to those who are pure in heart.

PSALM 73:1 ESV

Open your mouth and taste, open
your eyes and see—how good GOD *is.*
Blessed are you who run to him.

PSALM 34:8 MSG

LOST IN HIS LOVE

*As high as heaven is over the earth, so
strong is his love to those who fear him.
And as far as sunrise is from sunset, he has
separated us from our sins. As parents feel
for their children, GOD feels for those who
fear him. He knows us inside and out,
keeps in mind that we're made of mud.*

PSALM 103:11–14 MSG

God is love, and that love should influence every area of a Christian's life. Love is who God is—love is His very nature. God's love is more than a mother loves a child, or a husband loves a wife. No matter how you try to imagine it or measure it—there is no end to the depths of God's love for you.

Within our relationship with God there are times when it seems that God stands at a distance, longing for us to return His love by giving our all back to Him. It's when we give ourselves fully and completely to His will and plan for our lives that we can know His love completely.

As we come to God as His child and totally trust Him, it's then that we can find His deepest love for us, like a child who melts into her father's arms. The greatest experience a child of God can have is to become forever lost—safe and secure in His immeasurable, infinite, unending love.

God loves each of us as
if there were only one of us.

SAINT AUGUSTINE

God is love. Therefore love.
Without distinction, without calculation,
without procrastination, love.

HENRY DRUMMOND

Intense love does not measure,
it just gives.

MOTHER TERESA

I can only fly freely when I know there is a catcher to catch me. If we are to take risks, to be free, in the air, in life, we have to know that when we come down from it all, we're going to be caught, we're going to be safe. The great hero is the least visible. Trust the Catcher.

HENRI J. M. NOUWEN

Never be afraid to trust an unknown future to a known God.

CORRIE TEN BOOM

Warm me, your servant, with a smile;
save me because you love me.

PSALM 31:16 MSG

❀

Now make me completely happy!
Live in harmony by showing love
for each other. Be united in what you
think, as if you were only one person.

PHILIPPIANS 2:2 CEV

❀

Because Your lovingkindness is better
than life, my lips will praise You.

PSALM 63:3 NASB

He Is There

Lord, I don't know how many times I've stumbled or fallen and You were always there to catch me. As I remember those times, it builds my faith and trust in You. Those times provide a calm assurance of Your love. Thank You for being the One I can depend on no matter what. Amen.

See what kind of love the Father has given to us, that we should be called children of God; and so we are. The reason why the world does not know us is that it did not know him.

1 JOHN 3:1 ESV

"You can't worship two gods at once. Loving one god, you'll end up hating the other. Adoration of one feeds contempt for the other. You can't worship God and Money both. If you decide for God, living a life of God-worship, it follows that you don't fuss about what's on the table at mealtimes or whether the clothes in your closet are in fashion. There is far more to your life than the food you put in your stomach, more to your outer appearance than the clothes you hang on your body."

MATTHEW 6:24–25 MSG

Following Christ has nothing to do
with success as the world sees success.
It has to do with love.

MADELEINE L'ENGLE

At the end of the day people won't
remember what you said or did, they will
remember how you made them feel.

MAYA ANGELOU

Look for God. Look for God like a man
with his head on fire looks for water.

ELIZABETH GILBERT

*God showed his great love for us
by sending Christ to die for us
while we were still sinners.*

ROMANS 5:8 NLT

❁

We love Him, because He first loved us.

1 JOHN 4:19 AMP

❁

*Yet in all these things we are more than
conquerors through Him who loved us. For
I am persuaded that neither death nor life,
nor angels nor principalities nor powers,
nor things present nor things to come, nor
height nor depth, nor any other created thing,
shall be able to separate us from the love of
God which is in Christ Jesus our Lord.*

ROMANS 8:37–39 NKJV

Unconditional Love

God, thank You for loving me. Your love is uncomplicated and unconditional. In spite of all of my mix-ups and mess-ups, You wrapped Your arms around me and loved me. There is nothing I've done to cause You to love me, and nothing I can do to cause You to stop loving me. Thank You for loving me with a promise to never let me go. Amen.

"*Those who accept my commandments
and obey them are the ones who love me.
And because they love me, my Father
will love them. And I will love them and
reveal myself to each of them.*" Judas (not
Judas Iscariot, but the other disciple with
that name) said to him, "Lord, why are
you going to reveal yourself only to us and
not to the world at large?" Jesus replied,
"*All who love me will do what I say. My
Father will love them, and we will come
and make our home with each of them.
Anyone who doesn't love me will not obey
me. And remember, my words are not my
own. What I am telling you is from the
Father who sent me.*"

JOHN 14:21–24 NLT

PRAISING MY SAVIOR
ALL THE DAY LONG

*Bless the LORD, O my soul, and all
that is within me, bless his holy name!
Bless the LORD, O my soul, and forget
not all his benefits, who forgives all your
iniquity, who heals all your diseases, who
redeems your life from the pit, who crowns
you with steadfast love and mercy, who
satisfies you with good so that your youth
is renewed like the eagle's.*

PSALM 103:1–5 ESV

King David was a songwriter and a worshipper of the Lord who wrote seventy-plus psalms accredited to him in the Bible. Through these words of worship and praise, King David provides an open book of the thoughts, feelings, and intentions of his heart toward his Lord. Through failure and triumph, tragedy and great success, he lived life in praise to God. And there's much we can learn from the words King David penned.

Mankind was created to praise God (Isaiah 43:7; Matthew 21:16). Adam and Eve's disobedience and sin severed a perfect relationship between the Creator and His creation. Praise helps to restore a believer's relationship with God. The Creator resides in the praises of His people (Psalm 22:3). Praise silences the enemy, builds faith in the believer, and opens the heart to God. Praise isn't a single act you do, but a continual flow from the heart of man to God. Take time to praise the Lord by telling Him how you feel about Him. Let the heart of thanksgiving flow through you today.

*Through him then let us continually
offer up a sacrifice of praise to God, that is,
the fruit of lips that acknowledge his name.*

HEBREWS 13:15 ESV

❀

*Let everything that has breath and
every breath of life praise the Lord!
Praise the Lord! (Hallelujah!)*

PSALM 150:6 AMP

❀

*Praise the LORD, all you Gentiles!
Laud Him, all you peoples!
For His merciful kindness is great toward us,
And the truth of the LORD endures forever.
Praise the LORD!*

PSALM 117:1–2 NKJV

Worthy of Praise

Heavenly Father, I am celebrating You and all You are to me today. No matter where I am in life; no matter what attitude of my heart I have displayed, Your hands are always reaching toward me to bless me and encourage me. I am so thankful to know You. You are awesome and worthy of all praise! Amen.

*Let the word of Christ dwell in you
richly, teaching and admonishing one
another in all wisdom, singing psalms
and hymns and spiritual songs, with
thankfulness in your hearts to God.*

COLOSSIANS 3:16 ESV

*Hallelujah! O my soul, praise GOD!
All my life long I'll praise GOD,
singing songs to my God as long as I live.*

PSALM 146:1–2 MSG

*Give to the LORD the glory he deserves! Bring
your offering and come into his presence.
Worship the LORD in all his holy splendor.*

1 CHRONICLES 16:29 NLT

The greatest form of praise is the
sound of consecrated feet seeking
out the lost and helpless.

BILLY GRAHAM

In almost everything that touches our
everyday life on earth, God is pleased
when we're pleased. He wills that we be
as free as birds to soar and sing our
Maker's praise without anxiety.

A. W. TOZER

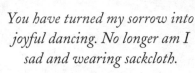

You have turned my sorrow into joyful dancing. No longer am I sad and wearing sackcloth.

PSALM 30:11 CEV

❁

Enter His gates with thanksgiving and His courts with praise. Give thanks to Him, bless His name.

PSALM 100:4 NASB

❁

Serve the LORD with gladness! Come into his presence with singing!

PSALM 100:2 ESV

All of My Days

Lord, my greatest desire is to please You. You gave me eternal life, and I want to give my life back to You each day. You consider me worthy of the greatest sacrifice by giving Your life for mine. I praise You. You are the ultimate example of selflessness and love. I will lift my voice in praise to You all of my days. Amen.

*And so faith, hope, love abide [faith—
conviction and belief respecting man's relation
to God and divine things; hope—joyful and
confident expectation of eternal salvation;
love—true affection for God and man,
growing out of God's love for and in us],
these three; but the greatest of these is love.*

1 Corinthians 13:13 amp